Saint Anthony of Padua

Saint Anthony of Padua

Fire and Light

Written by
Margaret Charles Kerry, FSP
and
Mary Elizabeth Tebo, FSP

Illustrated by
Ray Morelli

Pauline
BOOKS & MEDIA
Boston

Library of Congress Cataloging-in-Publication Data

Kerry, Margaret Charles, 1957–
    Saint Anthony of Padua : fire and light / written by
  Margaret Charles Kerry and Mary Elizabeth Tebo ;
  illustrated by Ray Morelli.
        p.   cm. — (Encounter the saints series ; 1)
    Summary: A brief biography of the much-loved
  thirteenth-century priest who lived and taught in   northern
  Italy and was recognised as a saint within a   year of his
  death.
    ISBN 0-8198-7019-6 (pbk.)
    1. Anthony, of Padua, Saint, 1195–1231—Juvenile
  literature.   2. Christian saints—Italy—Biography—
  Juvenile literature.   [1. Anthony, of Padua, Saint,   1195–
  1231.   2. Saints.]   I.Tebo, Mary Elizabeth. II. Morelli,
  Ray, ill.   III. Title.   IV. Series.
  BX4700.A6K49   1999
  282´.092—dc21
    [b]   99–17264
                                                       CIP

"P" and Pauline are registered trademarks of the Daughters
of St. Paul.

Copyright © 1999, Daughters of St. Paul

Published by Pauline Books & Media, 50 Saint Pauls
Avenue, Boston, MA 02130-3491.

Printed in the U.S.A.

www.pauline.org

Pauline Books & Media is the publishing house of the
Daughters of St. Paul, an international congregation of women
religious serving the Church with the communications media.

3 4 5 6 7 8   10 09 08 07 06 05

Encounter the Saints Series

Blesseds Jacinta and Francisco Marto
Shepherds of Fatima

Blessed Pier Giorgio Frassati
Journey to the Summit

Blessed Teresa of Calcutta
Missionary of Charity

Journeys with Mary
Apparitions of Our Lady

Saint Anthony of Padua
Fire and Light

Saint Bakhita of Sudan
Forever Free

Saint Bernadette Soubirous
Light in the Grotto

Saint Edith Stein
Blessed by the Cross

Saint Elizabeth Ann Seton
Daughter of America

Saint Frances Xavier Cabrini
Cecchina's Dream

Saint Francis of Assisi
Gentle Revolutionary

Saint Ignatius of Loyola
For the Greater Glory of God

Saint Isaac Jogues
With Burning Heart

Saint Joan of Arc
God's Soldier

Saint Juan Diego
And Our Lady of Guadalupe

Saint Julie Billiart
The Smiling Saint

Saint Katharine Drexel
The Total Gift

Saint Martin de Porres
Humble Healer

Saint Maximilian Kolbe
Mary's Knight

Saint Pio of Pietrelcina
Rich in Love

Saint Thérèse of Lisieux
The Way of Love

For other children's titles on the Saints,
visit our Web site: www.pauline.org

Contents

1

A LETTER AND A PROMISE

Twelfth-century Lisbon, Portugal, nestled on the banks of the Tagus River, breathed a quiet sigh as the year 1147 came to an end. With King Alfredo at its head, the Portuguese kingdom was at peace. But this happy situation was not to last.

In 1185, Sancho I took over the tiny kingdom of Portugal. Two thoughts filled his mind: build castles and become rich with gold. The people were taxed and taxed again until they could hardly buy food to eat. Their churches and monasteries were given to wealthy nobles and those loyal to the king. Life was difficult.

Just west of the great Cathedral of Lisbon, lived a young soldier named Martin and his wife Maria. Martin was in the king's service, so the couple's life was a little easier than that of most of their neighbors. Maria and Martin were good people with a deep religious faith. Martin often refused the privileges King Sancho offered him. He didn't want special favors that were not granted to others.

On August 15, 1195, Martin and Maria's first child was born. They named their baby boy Fernando. While all the family rejoiced over Fernando's birth, little did they know that in a few short years the entire world would join in the rejoicing. Little did they know that their Fernando would be remembered down through the centuries as Saint Anthony of Padua....

❖　❖　❖

"Martin! Martin!" called Maria. "Come in out of the heat. I have good news!"

"Coming, coming," a deep voice echoed back.

Martin stepped inside the cool home and dabbed at his forehead with a large handkerchief. Maria eyed her husband with pride. He carried himself with dignity and his bronzed skin and elegant mustache added to his distinguished look.

"Martin, your brother's written to say he'll be coming soon." Maria hugged her husband. "It will be good to see him again.

And he can give his blessing to the baby. I'm so excited!"

Martin's brother, Fernando, was a priest, happy with God and with his vocation. His occasional visits brought much joy and were always a good excuse for a family celebration.

"Now, Maria, stay calm," Martin gently chided. "When Fernando comes, he comes."

"The problem with you, my husband, is that you're *too* calm," Maria jokingly complained. "The baby's sleeping. I'm going to call one of the servants to prepare Fernando's room. Don't be late for supper."

The final days of summer were full ones for Maria. Caring for little Fernando and managing her household staff kept her busy, but she eagerly looked forward to Father Fernando's visit. Early one morning as she gazed out the window she spotted a familiar figure coming up the path.

"Martin...quick! It's your brother! Father Fernando is here!" Maria cried excitedly as she headed down the stairs, baby Fernando cradled in her arms.

Martin had already swung wide the front door. "It's so good to see you again, Fernando!" he exclaimed, embracing his brother.

"And it's very good to be here," Fernando grinned back.

Maria came up and gently placed the baby in Father Fernando's arms. "And who do we have here?" the priest half whispered. "He's beautiful. What have you named him, Maria?"

Maria was stunned. "Why, Father! Don't you remember? I wrote to you before he was born: 'If it's a boy, he will be named after you.'" Maria anxiously searched her husband's face. "Isn't that right, Martin?"

With a mischievous grin, the priest passed the baby back to Martin.

"Of course, Maria, of course. But I still say he looks just like me. Maybe we should have named him Martin after all."

Maria looked from brother to brother. "Shame on the two of you!" she finally sputtered. "You play jokes on me all the time!"

"Only because you take them so well, my dear," Martin laughed.

"Well, come have some breakfast now," Maria invited. "Your bag will be brought to your room, Father."

"Thank you, Maria, but first a blessing for my new nephew." Father Fernando raised his hand in the sign of the cross over the baby happily resting in Martin's muscular arms. "Little Fernando," he said, "I bless you in the name of the Father and of the Son and of the Holy Spirit. I also give you my promise. You will bring all people of this generation closer to God. You will search out those who do not yet know him and bring them the truth. The fire of your love will burn like a light in the darkness."

2

WHY?

There wasn't a game Fernando hadn't won or some trick he hadn't thought up. At least that's what Mama Maria thought as she kept a watchful eye on her children playing by a large tree.

"Giles! Capture the enemy!" Fernando yelled to his younger brother.

"Yes, Sir!" Giles snapped back.

Maria, their little sister, started to run, but her short legs couldn't carry her fast enough. She squealed as a pair of strong hands caught her.

"We've got the tyrant!" Giles cried.

"Good! Tie her to the tree!" Fernando commanded, tossing Giles a length of rope.

Fernando strolled over and frowned down at Maria. "Now don't move until we decide what to do with you." Then he and Giles huddled behind the tree to hold a conference. Within seconds they were back screaming: "We'll slay the enemy!"

By then little Maria had had enough of

this game. She let out a shrill shriek that sent Mama Maria flying out the door.

"Fernando! Giles! Untie your sister—right now!"

Fernando looked at his brother and nodded. "Giles, release the prisoner," he directed. The younger boy quickly unwound the rope according to Mama Maria's orders, and little Maria bounded into the house.

That night, Fernando quietly tiptoed to where his mother sat before the fireplace. "Mama...I'm really sorry about tying Maria to the tree."

Mama Maria didn't look up from her sewing. "Fernando," she said with a firm voice, "there's only one enemy, the devil. There's only one evil, and it is sin. Always remember that."

"Yes, Mama, I'll try." Fernando said nothing else. He went back to his room and slipped into bed.

Fernando tossed his mother's lesson around in his head for years. He liked sports, horseback riding and family get-togethers, but now, for some reason, his heart felt empty.

Giles was the first to notice the change in his brother. And he decided to find out what was going on.

"Hey, Fernando! How about going riding today? I'll get the horses. You get the lunch from Mama."

Fernando shrugged his broad shoulders. "All right. If you want to. I'll meet you by the stable in a few minutes."

The morning slipped into afternoon. Fernando and Giles stopped by a brook to eat. Giles tried to pry the problem from his brother. But Fernando just wouldn't talk. The day wore on. The two brothers raced their horses in a clearing. Then, with the sun starting to drop, they turned and headed home. As they steered their way down the winding path, Fernando caught sight of a small chapel.

"Giles, go on ahead of me. I'll catch up with you in a little while."

Fernando reigned his horse toward the chapel while Giles silently watched.

"I knew it was something like that!" Giles mumbled in a hurt tone. "I knew it." The younger boy spurred his mount on. His eyes were hot with tears.

Fernando slipped through the narrow chapel doors. Sunlight shimmered through the stained glass windows, dancing on the carved statues.

Fernando genuflected and knelt. Scenes

Fernando slipped through the narrow chapel doors.

of the wonderful day he'd spent with Giles crowded his mind. He sensed a certain peace, but it didn't last long. *All good things end,* he thought to himself. *How can I ever be happy with things that don't last? God is the only one who never changes. He's the only one who can give me real happiness.*

He bowed his head in prayer. *Lord, I give myself—all of myself—to you. I want to live with you and for you. Let this be our secret agreement.*

The minutes ticked by in silence. Fernando felt a quiet peace flood his soul. Getting up, he genuflected again, blessed himself and left the chapel. He mounted his horse and caught up the reins, starting back down the path toward home.

The sun had softened its rays and a warm evening glow had settled on the forest. By the time Fernando reached home, Giles was already brushing his horse in the stable.

"Giles!" Fernando cried, shaking his brother's shoulders, "I'm going to be a priest!"

"I knew it was something like that," Giles replied softly, "I knew it."

3

BREAKING THE NEWS

"When are you going to tell Mama and Papa?" Giles asked.

"In one week I'll be fifteen years old," Fernando thought out loud. "I'm almost a man! I'll tell them on my birthday. I'm just not sure yet how I'll say it."

"Well, where will you go to become a priest?" Giles prodded.

"I don't know," Fernando answered thoughtfully. "The Augustinian Fathers are very good. Maybe I'll go there."

Giles kicked the soft dirt of the stable floor. "I wish I were fifteen."

"You will be, Giles. Someday you'll wake up and be fifteen! But right now, I need your help to figure out how to tell Mama and Papa."

The boys plotted and planned together. Soon enough the day arrived.

Giles checked the positions of his parents, then reported back to Fernando.

"Mama's by the fireplace baking bread,

and Papa's sitting in his favorite chair. Now's the time!"

Fernando walked slowly into the living room. He could feel his knees trembling. His face was hot and flushed. *My throat's so dry. I hope I can talk.*

"Mama!" Fernando waited for her answer. A few seconds of silence followed. *Maybe she didn't hear me. I can still back out.*

But it was too late. Mama Maria looked up from her baking and smiled. "This is your favorite bread, Fernando. Come and try a piece!"

Fernando broke off a small piece of the soft, warm bread. "Mama, I have something to tell you."

"What's that, Fernando?"

"I...I want to be a priest. A priest like Uncle Fernando."

Papa Martin looked up from his reading. He and Mama Maria exchanged surprised glances.

"Are you sure about this?" Papa questioned, gazing steadily into Fernando's dark eyes.

"Yes. My mind is made up. I want to be a priest."

Mama Maria got up and kissed Fernando on the forehead. "Fernando, if you want to be a priest, be a good one. Don't hold anything back from the Lord. I'm sure you'll find much peace and joy in serving him."

Papa Martin joined in, "Wait till Father Fernando finds out! He'll hold a celebration as big as all of Portugal!"

Giles didn't want to be left out. After all, he'd helped Fernando plan how to break the news.

Giles peeked his head into the doorway. "Excuse me," he said in a grown-up manner. "When I'm fifteen—in two years—I'll have a big surprise for the family also!"

"Is that so?" Papa quipped. "Then we might as well continue the celebration until then!"

Fernando smiled. It was a perfect birthday.

4

AT HOME IN GOD'S HOUSE

Fernando grew more and more determined to enter the Augustinian monastery in Lisbon.

The whole family hid their tears whenever he was around, consoling each other with the reminder that Lisbon was close to home. They could visit the Monastery of Saint Vincent de Fora often.

Finally the day set for Fernando's entrance arrived. Fernando waved good-bye to everyone as he sat in the wagon beside his father. On the way, they spoke heart to heart. Fernando treasured his father's wise words of advice and realized more clearly than ever what a spiritual man he was.

The Augustinian monastery introduced the young teenager to a whole new world. He stepped into the routine with enthusiasm. Prayer, classes, study, work—everything would lead to his one goal—the priesthood.

Yet one craving gnawed at Fernando's heart. Often he would try to push it down, only to have it spring up again. Fernando loved the monastery, but he longed to bring the message of Jesus to every person on earth. How could he? The question haunted him.

Months passed. Then one morning there was a knock at his cell door. Fernando opened it. The brother standing there gave a slight bow and delivered his message, "Brother Fernando, Father Superior will see you now." The brother bowed again and disappeared down the hall.

Fernando walked hastily to Father Superior's cell. He had asked for an appointment with the superior, but now he felt a little nervous. He took a deep breath and knocked.

"Enter!" a voice within called.

Fernando opened the door.

"Come in, Fernando, come in."

The door clicked shut and the two religious stood face to face. The sunlight flooding the small cell gave the superior's graying hair a glint of gold.

"Please sit down," the superior invited, pointing to one of the room's two wooden chairs. A kind smile lit the older man's face as he himself sat down.

"You've been with us about two years

now, Fernando. Are you happy with our life?"

"Oh, yes, Father," Fernando slowly answered. "There's just one thing that bothers me. That's why I've asked to speak with you."

The superior leaned forward. "What is it that's troubling you, Fernando?"

"As you know, Father, my family and friends live nearby. It's easy for them to visit me and they visit often." Fernando's voice dropped. "Perhaps too often." The young monk lowered his eyes. "I'd like to ask your permission to transfer to another one of our monasteries where I can more fully give my life to Jesus in prayer and silence," he raised his eyes, "without so many...interruptions."

The superior nodded. "I can send you to Holy Cross Monastery in Coimbra," he said after a moment. "It's some distance from Lisbon and you will be able to continue your studies in theology and Sacred Scripture in peace." The older priest smiled as a look of relief lit the young monk's face. "Fernando, your faith is strong," he went on. "If you seek the Lord in your work and in your sufferings, I promise you a joy that will make you capable of great things."

The superior stood and pushed his chair

away from the desk—a sign that the meeting was over. "Pack your things this evening," he directed, laying his large hand on Fernando's shoulder. "Some of the monks are leaving for Coimbra tomorrow morning. You will accompany them. God be with you, Fernando!"

5

TOWARD THE CROSS

Fernando loved Holy Cross Monastery from the moment he first saw its tall, majestic steeple towering above him. There he happily placed himself under the guidance of Canon John, a famous scripture scholar who had previously taught at the University of Paris.

Fernando soon found himself immersed in the study of the Bible and the writings of Saint Augustine and other Fathers of the Church. He was eager to learn and wholeheartedly threw himself into his studies. But crosses are found everywhere in life. And they were not missing at Coimbra. Fernando quickly realized that his new monastery was split into two opposing groups.

King Alfonso II, the son of King Sancho, had cheated his sister out of her inheritance. Alfonso was excommunicated by the archbishop for having committed such a selfish deed. But in order to win his favor, some men had sided with King Alfonso against the archbishop and the Church. Unfortunately, one of these was the superior of Holy Cross Monastery. His love for wealth and riches caused the superior to seek his own pleasures. Some of the teachers and students at the monastery also followed his bad example.

The Pope tried to correct the superior's way of thinking, but the priest refused to give up siding with the king. Neither would he agree to give up his position of authority in the monastery. Instead, he wastefully and foolishly spent the monastery's money. It was a very difficult time. Those teachers and students who were obedient to the archbishop and the Church looked to Canon John for wisdom and courage.

Nine years of arguments and even serious injustices played their part in influencing Fernando's future. A lesson that was deeply engraved on his heart at this time was that riches and wealth can never make a person really happy. Fernando had joined the monastery to follow Jesus, not to live a comfortable life or be caught up in factions. He had been ordained a priest and he was trying his best to be a good one. But his heart was becoming more and more restless.

❖   ❖   ❖

A strong knock at the thick wooden door startled Fernando who was just beginning to doze off. He blinked and squinted at the dancing light of the candle burning in the hall. *It's very late.... There must be some trouble*, he thought.

The young priest was quickly on his feet, sliding back the heavy crossbeam that served as a bolt. The door squealed open. An oil lamp he held out revealed five friendly faces. One ventured to speak from the darkness.

"Good evening, Brother. We are Little Brothers, from Alenquer, near Lisbon. We follow Jesus after the manner of Francis of Assisi. We are journeying to Morocco, where we will tell the people about Jesus. Would we be able to spend the night at your monastery?"

Fernando smiled broadly. "Of course, Brothers, come in, come in!" He waved his hand toward the fireplace in a room off the hall. "Please sit and warm yourselves by our fire."

The friars shuffled in. One by one they introduced themselves to Fernando.

"I'm Berard."

"My name is Peter."

"I'm known as Adjutus."

"Accursius is my name."

"As for me, I'm called Otho."

"And I'm Father Fernando," their host responded.

Fernando couldn't help noticing how different these followers of Francis were from the priests and students at Holy Cross Monastery. As he sat with the little group huddled around the fire, he let his eyes wander over their habits—coarse, grayish tunics with hoods and rope belts. His gaze fell to their bare feet.

"I'll pray that your journey to Morocco is safe and fruitful, my Brothers," Fernando said slowly and with feeling.

"Thank you, Father. That is our prayer, too." Otho nodded. "And if it is not fruitful for those in Morocco, may it be fruitful for us through the grace of martyrdom!"

Fernando witnessed the glow of enthusiasm as each friar spoke. His own desire to preach Christ to the world flamed in his heart once more. But for now it could only remain that—a desire.

Fernando remained lost in thought for a few moments. Finally he rose to his feet. "You must be hungry after your travels, Brothers," he said kindly. "I'll bring some wine and fresh bread."

6

A New Beginning

The icy grip of winter melted into a perfect spring. Fernando sat studying in the monastery garden. Suddenly an urgent cry broke the silence. "Fernando! Fernando! There's sad news! Come quickly!"

Fernando slapped his book shut and jumped to his feet. "What news, Brother?"

"The Little Brothers of Francis who stayed here with us that night—" the monk before him struggled to catch his breath, "the ones who were on their way to Morocco—have been martyred! The Sultan himself ordered their execution."

"Who told you this?" demanded Fernando with tears in his eyes.

"Messengers from Don Giles, the king's brother. They rode in this morning. They also said that the bones of the five martyrs are being sent to us and will arrive within the month. Imagine! The relics will rest here in our own monastery. They are a gift to Canon John from Don Giles."

Fernando shook his head. "I can hardly believe what you're saying."

"It's true, Fernando. Berard tried to preach in the market place and he and his companions were arrested and thrown into prison. They were later released and ordered to return to their own country. Instead, they began preaching again. The Sultan was furious. He had them tortured in an attempt to make them give up the Faith. When he was unsuccessful, he gave the order that all five should be beheaded."

"But how did Don Giles get the bodies?" Fernando asked in a daze.

"Some Christians secretly placed the martyrs in a wooden box that night and carried it to the harbor. There was a ship docked there, ready to leave for Portugal in the morning. The Christians begged the captain to accept the box onto the ship so that the friars of Francis might rest in their homeland."

Fernando sobbed quietly, burying his face in his hands. He just couldn't get the martyred friars out of his mind.

Fernando spent long hours praying before the martyrs' relics once they arrived from Morocco. He remembered so clearly the cold wintry night when the friars had come to ask for shelter. Fernando struggled to know God's will. Should he remain a priest of the Augustinian Order or ask to become a friar with the Little Brothers? After many months, his secret tears bore fruit....

One day another group of Little Brothers knocked at the door of the monastery to beg alms and pray before the relics of their martyred brothers. Fernando happened to be serving as the porter that day and answered the door. He stared at the humble men. Suddenly he knew what he must do. *The time has come. It is the will of God that I go with them.*

Fernando took a deep breath.

"Please excuse me," he apologized, "I didn't mean to leave you standing outside. Come in, please come in. Our monastery will certainly give you alms. We only ask for your prayers in return. And I know you wish to pray before the relics of your martyred brothers. I will accompany you to the chapel where they rest."

On their way out of the chapel Fernando paused in the hall.

"Now, Brothers, I wish to ask a personal favor." He lowered his voice and went on, "I would like to become a follower of Francis so that I too may be sent as a missionary to Morocco."

The friars were dumbfounded. They could see that Fernando was well educated and living a comfortable life.

"Father," one of the friars finally stammered, "surely our Father Francis would rejoice at this request. Of course you may follow us. We will return for you in two days, after we have finished gathering alms."

Fernando lowered his head. "I'll be waiting for you," he said softly.

Fernando now had work to do. His first concern was Canon John. Fernando hurried to the older priest's cell. He knew Father John would be preparing his lesson for the following day.

A tired voice answered his knock. "Yes. Come in."

Fernando eased open the door and noiselessly closed it behind him. He looked with admiration at his teacher. Worry and suffering had taken their toll, but John was a strong man, capable of carrying large crosses.

"Sit down, Fernando," Canon John encouraged.

Fernando's words came tumbling out. "Father, in two days the Little Brothers will return to our monastery. And...," Fernando looked searchingly into the kind eyes of his teacher, "and I will go with them. I have asked the friars to accept me into their Order."

Father John bowed his head. A sigh trembled its way through his body. All of a sudden the priest appeared terribly old to Fernando. For long minutes he said nothing. Then, without looking up, Father John whispered, "Why? Why, Fernando?" He didn't wait for an answer, but raised his eyes to meet Fernando's. "You're not running away from the cross, are you?"

"No, Father, I'm running toward it," Fernando replied in a voice that was husky with pain.

Father John nodded. "Go then, with my blessing, my son," he murmured, "and pray for your poor father in Christ."

The only thing left to do was obtain the consent of his superior and community for the transfer. This was no easy feat, since Fernando was well-liked in the monastery, even by those who sided with the king. It was only with reluctance that the necessary permission was granted.

The two days passed swiftly. The news of Fernando joining the friars sparked blessings and arguments. Fernando breathed a sigh of relief when the followers of Francis finally returned and asked for him by name.

The monastery's two opposing groups of priests and students stood apart as they gathered to watch Fernando remove his white linen habit and replace it with the rough woolen tunic of the friars. Some members of the community wished him well. Others only stared in disbelief. Someone sarcastically called out, "Go on, Fernando! For sure you will become a saint now!"

Fernando answered quietly, "When you hear that I am a saint, my friend, go and praise God! I will do the same for you!"

The Little Brothers lost no time in returning with Fernando to their huts in an area called Saint Anthony of the Olives. All the members of the small community came out to welcome and greet their new brother. They showed him to his hut near their Chapel of Saint Anthony.

As he began his new life, Fernando was also given a new name—Anthony. It was the summer of 1220 and Anthony was twenty-five years old. He had been prepared by God for this new life through his teachers and through suffering. The love of Jesus burned in his heart. It was time now to light this same fire in others.

7

GOD'S PLANS

Anthony stayed with the friars at Saint Anthony of the Olives for a short time, learning about the Little Brothers' way of life. Soon enough he was assigned to Morocco as a missionary.

The ship creaked and listed leeward. "Drop anchor!" a sailor yelled. Anthony awoke to the sound of running steps on the deck above. He could hear Brother Philip breathing steadily in the bunk below him. He sat up. The air was heavy and rank with the smell of dead fish. The young priest pried open the wooden covering of the cabin's lone porthole. The merciless sun was about to rise. There was no movement of air—only overwhelming heat. Anthony felt strangely lightheaded and queasy. Propped up on his elbow, he continued to stare out the porthole. Through the haze the port of Morocco came into focus. It was already bustling with noise and activity. "I'm really here.... Thank you, God!" he whispered, wiping the perspiration from his forehead with his handkerchief.

Anthony shakily climbed down the few rungs of the bunk ladder. As he stood, he felt his knees weaken. *It must be the heat*, he thought to himself. *I'll feel better once I'm outside.* With great effort, he pulled himself up the narrow stairway leading to the deck. Sailors were everywhere, busily unloading the ship's cargo. Anthony finally managed to stop one. "Excuse me, Sir, but how many Christians live in Morocco?"

"Oh, I'd say about thirty-five, Father. It's not easy being a Christian in these parts. Difficult to keep yourself alive, you know!"

Anthony looked up to see Brother Philip climbing onto the deck. The tall, lanky youth spotted Anthony right away. The two friars soon found a quiet corner in which they said their prayers.

As the morning wore on, Anthony's head began to pound. By noon his eyes were blurred and a strange weakness threatened to overcome him. "When will the Christians come?" he mumbled to Philip.

"Soon, Father, soon," Philip soothed as he dabbed a wet rag over the priest's burning forehead.

Finally, a small but excited group of

"It's not easy being a Christian in these parts."

Christians appeared on the dock. Brother Philip called to them, while Anthony, lying on some bean sacks on the ship's deck, feebly tried to wave. He got up slowly. Leaning heavily on Philip's arm, he started to weave his way to the little group. But as the first hand went out to grasp his, everything went black and he crumpled to the deck.

"The fever's got him! Oh, God, don't let him die!" a woman wailed.

Some men of the group hastily fashioned a kind of stretcher out of some wooden poles and unfinished linen. Gently lifting Anthony onto the litter, they carried him down the gangplank to their cart.

When Anthony struggled to open his eyes, one of the older men bent over him with a sad smile.

"Father," he said softly, "maybe Morocco is not for you. Maybe your plans are not God's plans."

Maybe...maybe.... The words pierced Anthony's soul as he fell into a fitful sleep.

8

SHIPWRECK!

For a whole year Anthony lay in bed with a raging fever that came and went, leaving him too weak to do anything. Members of the tiny band of Moroccan Christians took turns helping to care for him. But oftentimes all they could do was keep him company during the long hours he spent in bed.

Spring brought cargo ships back into the Moroccan harbor. The Christians urged Anthony to board one of the vessels returning to Portugal. His health had refused to improve and everyone feared for his life. It was decided that Brother Philip would accompany him back to their homeland.

After tearful good-byes, Anthony, supported by Philip's strong arms, climbed the gangplank of one of the ships. His hands clutched the small parcel of fresh bread and fruit his friends had packed for him.

Exhausted and still burning with fever, Anthony knelt in the friars' assigned cabin before a small cross he had made.

"Jesus, my Master," he whispered, "I give myself to you, mind, heart and will. Use me to spread the light of your Gospel. Let me give you all that I possess—nothing less. Nothing less."

❖   ❖   ❖

Anthony lay motionless on his bunk. The steady beating of waves against the ship's hull was mercifully lulling him to sleep. Philip decided to go up on deck to pray.

The air was unusually thick and heavy. Suddenly the seaman at watch let out a desperate scream, "A storm...up ahead! Lower the sails...secure the hatches!.... Drop anchor!.... Now!"

The great ship rolled from side to side. Anthony woke with a start. Something was very wrong. He struggled up to the deck. The scene that met his eyes shocked him. Angry clouds hung dangerously low, blurring the division between sky and sea. Streaks of lightning slashed the eerie darkness and swelling waves were beginning to break over the prow. Philip came running to Anthony's side as another jolt of the ship threw him against the railing. The brother clutched at the wet wool of the priest's habit. "Father!" he shouted over the roar of the wind, "we must get back to the cabin!"

Around dawn the following day a sickening scraping sound shook the vessel. With a great heave it lurched to one side. Seconds later a burly sailor threw open the door of the friars' cabin. He was drenched and trembling with cold, his hair white and stiff with salt. Anthony tried to focus his eyes on the man. "How can I help you, my brother?" he whispered.

"Father! We've run aground...we're taking in water! We must abandon ship!"

The sailor read the terror in young Philip's eyes and immediately saw that Anthony was too weak to walk. Without a word he scooped the sick priest into his brawny arms and headed for the ladder. Philip followed on his heels.

Within minutes all three found themselves in the water. Thankfully, the shore was very close, and with the strong tide in their favor the captain, crew and friars were soon washed up on the sand.

9

THE MEETING

Anthony sat propped against a tree while Philip struggled to light a fire on the beach. Their sailor friend, who had gone in search of villagers, soon came running back with a dark-haired man and some good news. "We're in Italy, Sicily to be exact," he sputtered between breaths. "The townspeople say that your friars have a place a few miles up the shore in Messina. This farmer has offered to bring you there in his cart."

"Blessed be God who gives the swallows a nest!" Anthony exclaimed.

Philip and the sailor eased Anthony into the cart and the farmer covered him with a heavy blanket.

Anthony's gaze traveled from the captain to each of the crew members. "I will remember you all before the altar of our good God," he gratefully promised. Philip hopped in beside him and the farmer goaded his horses into action.

❖ ❖ ❖

Near the end of spring the friars of Francis held a meeting in North Umbria, the beautiful Italian region around Assisi. Many friars from different parts of the Holy Roman Empire attended. They knew it was probably the last time they would see Francis, their beloved father, again. Anthony made the strenuous trip, too, although his illness had left his eyes and heart very weak.

The friars came in ones and twos, in groups and then in throngs over the mountains and hills of Umbria to Francis' village of Assisi, nestled between the thick forests and silver lakes.

Anthony, with the help of a cane, started to climb the last hill but had to stop to catch his breath. A large hand gently reached out to support him.

"You look like you've come a long way, Brother. My name is Father Gratian. Could I help you up the hill?"

"Thank you, Father. I'm Father Anthony from Portugal. On our way back to Portugal from Morocco another friar and I were blown off course and landed in Sicily. So perhaps I haven't had to travel as far as some of the other brothers to get here. The will of God can even use hurricanes to make straight our crooked ways."

Gratian nodded and smiled. The two men continued their conversation as they stepped into the line leading to Francis's hut. When their turn came, Gratian introduced Anthony to Francis. "Anthony is from Portugal, Father Francis. He entered our Order about a year ago and was missioned to Morocco, but had to return because of ill health."

Francis looked intently at Anthony and extended his frail hand in welcome. Then, being too weak to speak aloud, he whispered something into the ear of Brother Elias, who sat beside him. "Our Father Francis asks God to light your path that you in turn may light the way for others," Elias repeated.

Anthony and Gratian bent low and Francis traced the sign of the cross on each of their foreheads. Then it was time to move on.

Father Gratian led the way to one of the clusters of crude huts that dotted the hillsides. With 3,000 friars in the town, there just wasn't room enough in the homes of the townspeople. Most of the friars took shelter in tiny huts that they had constructed of clay and twigs. And what about food? Someone had said that there were only a few loaves of bread and three sacks of fruit in the entire "camp." It was nowhere near enough to feed so many hungry men who had been walking for days. But Francis knew better. He urged his friars to trust God who would take care of all their needs.

Another holy man, whom we now know as Saint Dominic, was passing through Assisi at this time. He stopped to see Francis. Dominic was amazed at the great number of friars who had gathered for the meeting. "How are you going to feed your Brothers, Francis?" he asked. "Do you have a store of food and supplies?"

Francis just smiled. "God will provide, Dominic, for all of us! Please spend the night with us so you and I can talk."

Soon after Francis had spoken, a large cart pulled by a donkey came to a halt before his hut. A farmer jumped down from its seat and pulled back its canvas covering. To everyone's surprise, the cart was loaded with heaps of grapes, crates of homemade cheese, milk, fresh bread, wine, olive oil, vegetables and roasted chickens. There were even pastries for dessert!

The man looked around and gave a hearty laugh. "What's the matter, don't you know how to eat?" he teased. That broke the spell. The friars scrambled to unload the food God had so generously sent them through the kind farmer.

When everything had been set out for the meal, the peasant climbed back onto his seat. "This is just a sample of what's to come," he happily announced. "The people of Assisi have noticed you. We've sent our children to count you so that we could bring enough food for all. See—" he beamed, pointing to a trail of carts appearing over the crest of the hill, "you will have plenty to eat for as long as you are with us."

10

ANOTHER "YES"

The friars were inspired by what they had learned and experienced at their special meeting with Francis. New superiors had also been elected for the different provinces. Now it was time to begin the long journeys back to their monasteries. But Anthony, who wasn't well known, had been left without an assignment. He knew that Father Gratian was one of the provincial superiors. He finally decided to approach him. "Would I be able to come with you, Father?" Anthony quietly asked.

Gratian looked thoughtful for a moment. Anthony was still pale and thin. Taking him might mean a sacrifice for his monastery, but Gratian could see goodness and sincerity in the young priest's eyes. And that was enough for him. "Yes, come. Come, Anthony," he warmly invited.

As the two friars walked along they talked and prayed. "Thank you for accepting me, Father Gratian," Anthony started out. "I'll try not to be a burden to you. In fact, with your permission, I'd like to live as a hermit."

"A hermit? Well now. Monte Paolò, where you'll be staying, is a beautiful place," replied Gratian, "a kind of Garden of Eden that will lift your thoughts to our Creator. I don't think there will be any problem with your living as a hermit there. No, no problem at all, Anthony," he smiled.

The two friars reached Monte Paolo in late afternoon. They were warmly welcomed by Friars Louis, Joseph, and Giaccomo, the guardian or superior of the little community. It was a joyful reunion and supper that evening lasted longer than usual. The brothers were very anxious for news of their Father Francis and the recent meeting. And Gratian and Anthony were only too happy to answer all their questions.

After Father Gratian left early the next morning, Giaccomo took Anthony on a tour of his new home. He showed him the different garden plots, the many little mountain springs and the caves where the brothers prayed and sometimes stayed.

"Whose cave is that?" Anthony inquired, pointing to a small, damp grotto carved into the side of the mountain.

"No one's," Giaccomo answered absent-mindedly. "We use it for storage. You know, tools and things."

"May I have it for my room?" Anthony quietly asked. "It would be perfect," he added with a grin.

"Your room?" Giaccomo repeated in surprise. "Well, if that's what you want, I suppose so."

"Thank you, Brother! Thank you very much!"

Days were peaceful at Monte Paolo and passed before they could be counted. The warmer weather brought with it new work in the fields. It also brought the little community an invitation to attend an ordination ceremony in the nearby town of Forli.

The ordination turned out to be a wonderful celebration. Several young men from Father Dominic's Order of Friars Preachers were ordained to the priesthood along with some of the Little Brothers. Besides the bishop, there were many priests and brothers from both Orders in attendance. Everyone was enjoying themselves. And Anthony was happy for the chance to see Father Gratian again. But halfway through the meal that followed the ceremony, a problem arose.

It was the custom, on such an occasion, for one of the priests to give a spiritual talk to the group. Father Gratian realized it was time for the speech. But where was the speaker? He decided to find out. "Please excuse me a moment, Your Excellency," he murmured to the bishop as he pushed his bench back from the table. He quickly singled out the provincial superior of the Friars Preachers in his white habit and black cape. "Father, who has been appointed to give the talk?" Gratian asked in an anxious tone. "I'd like to introduce him now."

The provincial's gray eyebrows shot up in surprise. "No one asked us to speak, Father. We thought one of your friars would be giving the talk."

Gratian felt his face getting hot. "But..." he stammered, "we have no one prepared."

"Neither do we," the white-robed friar answered, nervously stroking his beard. "Why don't you try asking for a volunteer?"

"That's a good idea," Gratian nodded. "A good idea."

Father Gratian moved up and down the rows of priests, quietly explaining the embarrassing situation. But one after another came the answers.

"Oh no!"

"Not me!"

"I'm not ready to give a talk."

Gratian was starting to feel panicky. He stopped and scanned the room. Suddenly his eyes met Anthony's. In a moment he was beside him. Bending low he quietly commanded, "Father Anthony, say whatever the Holy Spirit inspires you to say!"

Anthony obediently stood up. All eyes were on him as he calmly walked to the front of the room. He bowed his head in silent prayer as whispers passed up and down the long table. Who was this friar? Where was he from?

Anthony began softly, with a slight quiver in his voice, "My Brothers, fire enflames whatever it touches but never lessens in power." His dark eyes flashed and his voice grew steady and deeper. "So, too, the Holy Spirit, when he enters a soul sets it on fire with love and then sends it out to enkindle others. Today we will consider the fire in these words of Scripture, 'Christ became obedient unto death, even to death on a cross.'" The words flowed effortlessly and Anthony held his audience spellbound. Many of the priests and brothers found themselves moving up closer so as not to miss anything he was saying. The listeners soon lost all track of time. When Anthony finished, a great hush fell upon the room. The bishop was smiling and nodding approvingly. Gratian felt an unexplainable excitement in his heart. He made his way to Anthony and grasped him by the shoulders. "My Brother," he half whispered, "our Lord has inspired your words and all of us through them. I believe that he wants you to be the lamp placed on the lamp stand. I mean, Anthony, that you must now go out and preach—to all of Italy."

Anthony lowered his head. Once again he was being asked to leave all he knew and loved. Once again he was being asked to set out for the unknown. And once again he answered "yes" in his heart.

11

RESCUE

"Father! Father!"

Anthony turned to see a young boy running down the dusty road toward him.

"Father!"

"Slow down," Anthony called back. "I'll wait for you right here. I promise."

When the boy caught up to him, Anthony pointed to a tree. "Let's sit down for a few minutes so you can catch your breath."

The boy nodded and the two sat in the cool shade.

"My mother heard you were coming and sent me to walk with you, Father," the boy panted. "The people of North Umbria don't like priests, you know. It's not safe to travel alone."

"What's your name?" Anthony broke in.

"Mario," the boy replied.

"Thank you for coming to keep me company, Mario. Tell me, what are the people of North Umbria like?"

"My mother says they're very poor—like us. They think all priests are rich. So they don't want to listen to them or help them either." Mario stopped, looking confused. "Are you rich, Father? You don't look rich!"

Anthony laughed softly. "No. No, I'm not rich, Mario. But I do have a treasure to share with the people of North Umbria."

The boy's brown eyes grew wide. "You do?" he asked. "What is it? Can I have some, too?"

"The treasure is Jesus and his Church. And yes, you will be the first to receive something of this treasure," Anthony promised.

At that the young priest's right hand disappeared into his habit's deep pocket. It came back out holding a little cross of polished wood. "For you," Anthony said, pressing the cross into the boy's hand. "Jesus died on the cross for you. It's a reminder of how much he loves you."

Mario couldn't take his eyes off the cross. It was the first holy gift he had ever received. "Thank you, Father," he whispered, "thanks a lot."

"Well, we'd better be going," Anthony observed. "It's getting late and we still have to find a place to sleep for the night."

"Don't worry, Father. My mother has spoken with a lady in town. She'll be very happy to give us supper and let us spend the night at her house. We'll go there now."

It rained hard during the night but the sky was a deep and cloudless blue the next morning as Mario waved good-bye to Anthony. The boy started on his way home, happily clutching his cross. *The people will like Father Anthony...I just know they will!* he thought to himself. *They'll see how much he really loves God and practices what he teaches.*

Setting out in the direction of the church, Anthony wondered exactly how and where he could begin to preach the Gospel of Jesus to the townspeople. An angry yell suddenly interrupted his thoughts. "You stupid animal!...good for nothing but trouble, that's what you are!" Up ahead of him, at a turn in the road, Anthony could see a farmer whose ox was stuck in the thick, orange mud.

Anthony stepped up his pace. "May I help you?" he called to the farmer, as he rolled up his sleeves. The red-faced farmer turned from the ox to Anthony. He stared him up and down. "Are you a priest?" he gruffly demanded.

"Yes, I am," Anthony answered with a smile.

The farmer pulled out a huge bandanna and began mopping his face. "You might get dirty," he warned in a sarcastic tone.

"That's fine! I'm used to it!" Anthony countered.

Priest or no priest, the farmer needed help and there was no one else around.

"All right. Grab his harness and pull from the front," he grudgingly directed.

After a few minutes of struggle, the animal was finally freed. With the last pull Anthony found himself knee-deep in the mud. The farmer broke into a grin and Anthony let out a loud laugh.

"A little water will wash the mud off," cackled the farmer.

"Just like the sacrament of Penance cleanses our souls!" Father Anthony exclaimed.

The farmer was silent.

"Tell me, my friend, how far from here is the church?" Anthony prodded.

The farmer hesitated. He seemed to be deciding something of great importance. "Climb up!" he finally ordered, pointing to the seat beside him. "The church is about five miles away."

As they rode along, Anthony tried to find out why the people of the area were so hostile to priests. Little by little the truth came out—the townspeople had been confused by false teachings about Jesus and the

"A little water will wash the mud off,"
cackled the farmer.

Church he founded. Anthony realized that the best way he could help them was through prayer and good example.

"This is it," the farmer said as they finally pulled up before the church, a graceful building of cut stone, boasting a bronze bell in its high tower. A cheerful little garden surrounded it on three sides.

"It's beautiful!" Anthony admired. Then, looking straight into the eyes of the farmer, he asked quietly, "Will I see you at Mass tomorrow?"

The farmer quickly looked away. *What is it about this priest?* He thought to himself. *He seems to see right into my soul.* "There are about five people who come to church," the farmer answered roughly, "I'm not one of them. Thanks for your help."

The next morning Anthony rang the church bell loud and long. He heard a few confessions then went back to the sacristy to vest for Mass. As he walked to the altar he looked over his tiny congregation. The five churchgoers had been joined by a sixth— there in the very back was the farmer.

"*Thank you, my Lord,*" Anthony prayed in his heart. "*Thank you.*"

12

GO TEACH, PREACH

Father Gratian carefully unfolded the slip of paper in his hand. He held it up to the light and read: *To Anthony, I, Brother Francis, send greetings. It would please me, my Brother, if you would teach the friars Sacred Scripture and theology. Take care, however, that in such studies they always uphold the spirit of holy prayer as it is contained in our Rule. Peace and all good. Francis.*

Gratian smiled and handed the note to Anthony.

"My prayers go with you, Anthony. The Lord has given you great success in teaching the faith to the people of northern Italy. So many have returned to the sacraments. Many others have asked to be baptized. May God continue to bless you in this new assignment."

"Thank you, Father Gratian. Thank you for all you've done for me," Anthony said quietly.

"Remember, now, that although Brother Francis has a great respect for theologians, he's never wanted any of us to seek knowledge out of curiosity," Gratian gently warned. "He prefers the practice of virtue to any studies which could tempt us to think we're wiser than others."

"I'll remember that," Anthony promised, "and I'll remind the brothers that we study only to learn more about Jesus and to make him loved. Many of those who oppose the teachings of the Lord are educated men. We must study to be able to point out their errors and teach the real truth in love."

Sent to the city of Bologna, Anthony helped to organize a house of studies where he taught the friars Sacred Scripture and the truths of the Catholic faith. After the hours spent in the classroom, he would ask the brothers to go out and preach to the people. "Now share what you've received!" he'd encourage them. Whenever he wasn't teaching, Anthony himself went out to preach, too.

Once a prominent person of the town of Rimini wrote to Anthony and begged him to come and preach there. People had fallen away from the faith and confusion was spreading throughout the area.

Anthony went to his superior with the

letter. "Father Guardian, I could reach Rimini in three days, preach for a week and then return." There was an earnestness in his voice as he added, "May I have your permission to make the trip?"

The guardian studied Anthony. It was clear that the young priest was not well. His legs and ankles were painfully swollen and his face was pale and drawn. *He's never fully recovered from that illness he contracted in Morocco*, the superior thought. But it was Anthony's eyes that caught and held the older priest's attention, those eyes that seemed to burn with a secret fire. The guardian knew that fire—the fire of love.

"You may go, Anthony, but on one condition," the superior answered thoughtfully.

"What's that, Father?"

"I'd like Brother Albert to accompany you."

"Thank you, Father!" Anthony exclaimed. "I'll notify Brother Albert right away. He's one of my students."

The two missionaries received a very cold reception in Rimini. Sometimes a crowd would gather to listen to Anthony, but most people came only out of curiosity. As soon as Anthony began to urge them to follow Jesus and obey his Church, heads would wag, many would scoff and the gathering would begin to break up.

When this happened again one day Albert grew impatient. "Father Anthony!" he protested, "Why don't we just pack up and go home? These people don't want to listen to you. We're not doing any good. We're just wasting time!"

Anthony smiled as the crowd continued to thin. "Before we leave, let's go and speak to the fish, Albert. Maybe they will listen."

Albert was puzzled, but he obeyed. The two friars turned and headed for the river. A few of the most curious onlookers followed at a safe distance. "Who knows what this strange priest will do next?" they joked.

Anthony stopped by the river's edge. In a voice that rang with authority, he shouted, "Hear the Word of God, you fish of the sea!" There was a sudden splashing sound as hundreds of fish of all shapes and sizes surfaced near the shoreline, their shiny heads bobbing up and down in the gentle waves. "My brothers, the fish," Anthony continued in a loud voice, "give praise to your Creator! God has honored you in so many ways. When the flood came upon the earth, you did not drown. When Jesus lived among us, he loved to preach near you...." By now the townspeople, who minutes before had turned their backs on Anthony and Albert, were running excitedly toward the river. "A miracle! A miracle!" someone yelled. Many people had already fallen to their knees in the wet sand. Others were weeping loudly. "Blessed be the eternal God!" Anthony cried out. "His fish honor him more than his people who refuse to listen to his word!"

Brother Albert could feel his heart racing as the people thronged Anthony begging to go to confession. One man returned to the sacrament after thirty years.

It was a day neither Albert nor Rimini would ever forget.

13

To France

"God be with you!" the young friars clustered around the door of the monastery called. "And bring our greetings to the Brothers in Parma," the superior reminded, "they'll be expecting you tonight." Anthony and his companion turned and waved.

The journey on foot from Bologna over the mountains and into France would be a tiring one, especially for Anthony. His legs were now scarred with painful ulcers and his breathing was becoming increasingly difficult because of the water collecting around his lungs. But obedience was calling him to preach in France. And Anthony was happy to go.

As the friars walked along, Anthony remembered the advice of their Father Francis, "When the friars go through the world, they shall take nothing with them along the way, neither purse nor wallet, nor bread, nor money, nor staff. And whatever house they enter, let them first say, 'Peace to this house!' and they should remain in the same house and eat and drink what the people have." *Yes,* he thought to himself, *this is our way of joyful penance and poverty.*

After a few days of traveling, the friars came to the foot of the Alps. Then they began the final long trek up this mountain range that divides Italy and France. Another day's journey would bring them to the French town of Annecy.

It was growing dark as they reached the outskirts of Annecy. Purple clouds rolled overhead, threatening to spill their rain at any minute. The chilling wind had picked up and was whistling about them. Anthony and his companion hugged their thin cloaks as they came up to a large house. Anthony knocked at the heavy door.

Minutes passed before a servant answered. She opened the door a crack.

"What do you want?" she demanded.

"Peace be to your house," Anthony replied calmly in French. "We are friars, begging for bread."

"Wait here. I'll have to ask." The girl turned abruptly, leaving the door ajar.

"Who is out in such dreadful weather?" the friars heard a voice from within call.

"Just some friars, Madame, begging for bread."

"Asking only for bread and not for shelter?" the surprised voice was coming closer. Suddenly the door swung fully open.

"Who are you?" a well-dressed woman asked.

"We are God's poor beggars, my lady, followers of Francis of Assisi," Anthony explained, "We've traveled many miles to offer the Good News of Jesus to anyone who will listen. We're on our way to our friary in Arles, but we have no more bread."

"Brothers, please come in out of the storm," the woman urged. "By all means you must take something to eat and spend the night here."

"God will bless your kindness," Anthony smiled. "He's never outdone in generosity."

"My servant will prepare you a hot meal, Brothers, and see to it that you have everything you need," the lady of the house said with authority. Even as she spoke the servant girl headed off to the kitchen. "In the meantime, come and warm yourselves by the fire."

"Thank you, my lady," the brothers answered gratefully.

The noble woman rose early the next morning. She wanted to be sure that the servant had a hearty breakfast ready for her guests. The friars soon heard loud voices coming from the kitchen.

"But, Madame...."

"You take very good care of me. I'm sure getting up early will do me no harm, no harm at all," the mistress of the house was protesting.

The servant mumbled something as Anthony and his companion appeared in the doorway. The friars greeted the women and sat down to breakfast with the lady of the house. They spoke of their missionary trip to France as they ate.

"We can't thank you enough for your kindness," Anthony said as he pushed his chair back from the table. "But we must be leaving now. We have a long trip ahead of us."

Realizing that the friars couldn't be persuaded to stay any longer, the good woman turned to Anthony. "Father," she asked, "would you please remember me and my household—especially the child I now carry—in your prayers?"

"Of course," smiled Anthony. After some moments of silence, he added. "You can be very happy about the child soon to be born, my lady. God has revealed to me that he will join our Order and become a martyr. He will encourage many others to witness to Jesus as well."

The prophecy came true. The woman gave birth to a baby boy, whom she and her husband named Philip. When Philip grew up he joined the Little Brothers. Eventually he went as a missionary to the Holy Land. There, after years of hard work, he and many other Christians were thrown into prison by the Sultan. They were ordered to give up their Christian faith or die. Philip encouraged his companions to remain strong and die for Christ. He asked to be the last one to be put to death so that he could pray with and help the Christian martyrs until the end. And that is exactly what happened.

14

THE BOY AND THE BOOK

More and more of the Christians of France were becoming confused and falling away from the practice of their faith. They worried Pope Honorius III. He wrote letters to several French bishops begging them to find ways to instruct and assist the people. He also wrote to the University of Paris and asked the students there to see what they could do to help the situation.

Anthony took all of this to heart. He spent much time preaching in France. Whenever he entered a town he went straight to the church and prayed for the people who would hear him speak. He spent long hours hearing their confessions. He even healed many. As he was about to leave a town, he would encourage the people, "Jesus is waiting for you in the Blessed Sacrament. He wants to give you his love and receive your love in return. Visit him often. Don't disappoint him!"

Besides preaching, Anthony lived for some time in the French cities of Montpellier and Toulouse. There he taught Sacred Scripture to his fellow friars. They would, in turn, go out and teach the people.

At the time Anthony lived, books were scarce and very expensive. Scholars took notes and later taught from their notebooks. Over a period of time, these notebooks became very precious. And so it's easy to understand why Anthony felt very bad one afternoon when he discovered that his notebook on the Psalms was missing. He felt even worse when he learned that a young novice had also disappeared from his monastery that day.

Anthony knelt in the silence of his tiny cell. He covered his face with his hands. "My Lord," he prayed, "send them both back, the boy and the book."

Sunset came and went. The stars were already out when Anthony heard a soft rapping on his cell door. He unlatched it and drew it open. In the glow of the candlelight stood the silhouette of the fugitive novice, the missing notebook clutched in his trembling hands. Anthony grasped the young man by the shoulders. "Thank God you're safe!" he exclaimed. "Come in, come in."

The novice fell to his knees. The fearful

"Thank God you're safe! Come in, come in."

eyes that looked up at Anthony were red and puffy.

"Why did you run away?" Anthony gently prodded.

"Because I was homesick. I don't think I belong here, Father." The novice stared at the floor. "I'm not holy like the others, like you. I never will be." The boy's shadow was quivering now. "I was going to sell your notebook, Father," he sobbed.

Noiselessly Anthony knelt before the novice. He bowed until his head nearly touched the wooden floor. "None of us is holy," he whispered. "We are all sinners. We all need God's love and mercy. And he wants so much, so much to give them to us—" he raised his head. "To give them to you." Anthony was pleading now. "Will you let him?"

The young man couldn't speak. Tears were streaming down his cheeks. He nodded.

"Don't be afraid," Anthony reassured him. "I forgive you and so does the Lord. Never again doubt that you are where you belong. And never again doubt that the Lord loves you very much. Will you promise me that?"

The novice nodded again. Anthony smiled as the boy pressed the notebook into his hands. He stood and raised the novice to his feet.

"Good night my young Brother," he said quietly. "Go in much peace."

15

ANTHONY OF PADUA

After the time he spent teaching and preaching in and around Toulouse, Anthony was chosen to be Father Guardian in Le Puy en Velay, a city about 175 miles away. This new assignment required him to visit all the monasteries of the Little Brothers in the area, always walking from place to place. Traveling became his real cross. The swelling in his legs and feet never went down. The water collecting around his lungs made it more and more of a struggle for him to breathe. But Anthony was on fire with love of God. He never mentioned his sufferings. He never complained.

Soon after Francis died in Assisi in October of 1226, Anthony, now thirty-two years old, was called back to Italy. He set out on the journey with another friar. Their sandals kicked up little clouds of dust as they walked the dirt road leading over the mountains. Climbing the first peaks of the Alps, Anthony stopped and turned for a last look at the beautiful country he would never see again. "Good-bye, France," he murmured, raising his hand in the sign of the cross, "may the Lord bless and preserve you... always."

The friars of the monastery nearest the Italian-French border were keeping an anxious lookout. Excited cries of welcome rang out as Anthony and his traveling companion finally came into view. "Father Anthony! Father Anthony! Welcome home! Welcome also to you, Brother!"

One of the friars hurriedly brought out a chair. Anthony sat down heavily. His chest was heaving and his face was gray. It was obvious that he wasn't well. The brothers gathered around him in concern. Someone brought him a drink of water. After a few long minutes his breathing grew steadier.

A young friar impulsively asked, "Tell us all about France, Brothers..."

"That would take some time!" Anthony replied with a grin. Then his face became serious. "Were any of you with our Father Francis when he passed into the arms of the Lord?" A hush fell over the little group. "Yes," one of the older friars quietly replied, "I was among the Brothers called when our Father Francis was dying. Even in the cold he asked to be placed on the damp ground.

He wanted to welcome Sister Death detached from all earthly goods. His was a holy death, so peaceful, as we wish ours to be. Truly he is now with the Lord."

Anthony's dark eyes were wet with tears. "Thank you, Brother," he whispered. "We didn't receive much news in France."

❖   ❖   ❖

Much important work awaited Anthony in Italy. He was named provincial superior of the northern section of the country. This gave him the responsibility of looking after many communities of friars. He also continued teaching the younger friars, and preaching and hearing confessions in the towns and villages.

Anthony often went to preach in the city of Padua, a city whose people never seemed to be at peace. The citizens of Padua and those of nearby Verona constantly squabbled over land and money. Anthony patiently taught them how to find true happiness, reminding them about heaven and stressing that no one can love God and money at the same time. He sincerely loved the people and they loved him.

Once, when two wealthy men were fighting in the street, it was Anthony who broke up the argument. "Whoever feels himself a prisoner of greed should think of the Son of God," Anthony calmly pointed out. "He should remember how Jesus was wrapped in swaddling clothes and laid in a manger," he continued as the culprits' faces grew redder and redder. "Jesus had nowhere to lay his head except the cross on which he died. Tell me, now, how can you two be fighting over land which happens, in the first place, to belong to God?" he gently chided. A murmur ran through the crowd that had gathered. Everyone had to agree that Anthony was right. The wealthy nobles went home in silence.

In 1230, Anthony was relieved of his duty as provincial superior. He went to live permanently at the monastery in Padua. He continued walking the streets and preaching, spreading peace wherever he went. He often had to preach in the town square or in open fields because there was no church large enough to hold the crowds that came to hear him. When he finished a sermon, he would spend long hours hearing confessions, often going most of the day without eating.

The fever Anthony had suffered years before now kept him awake at night. His hands, stomach, legs and feet were swollen beyond shape. And it was becoming harder and harder for him to breathe. Anthony felt that the end of his life was near. Only one fear troubled him now—that of being a burden to his brothers.

16

ONE LAST JOURNEY

Just after Lent, in 1231, Anthony asked permission to go and live in a small hut among the friars of Camposampiero, a village not too far from Padua. He wanted to pray in solitude and prepare to meet Jesus, his Master. His superiors agreed. They even sent two friars to accompany and assist him.

June 13 dawned hot and humid. As always, Brothers Roger and Luke helped Anthony to the noon meal. But something was different today. Today Anthony's hands shook as he tried to pick up his bread. Today he suddenly felt himself falling backward off his bench. He gripped the edges of the table.

Brother Luke jumped to his feet. "Father, perhaps you should lie down for a few minutes...."

"Yes, I think so," Anthony feebly replied. Attempting to stand, he immediately collapsed into the arms of the friars beside him. After the worried friars had carried him to bed, Roger and Luke remained with him. Anthony whispered weakly to Brother

Roger, "Maybe I should return to the monastery in Padua. I will only be a bother to you in this out-of-the-way place."

"Don't talk like that, Father!" Roger protested. "We're very happy to take care of you. Stay here. The country air will do you good."

Anthony turned his head. "Luke, could you please get the sermons I was working on?"

"I'll be right back with them, Father."

As Luke left the hut Anthony reached for Roger's hand. He squeezed it. "I'm dying, my Brother," he said quietly, "and I would very much like to die in Padua." He gripped Roger's hand. "Would you get a wagon ready to take me home?" His voice was trembling now. "Forgive me for all the trouble I'm causing," he begged.

"There's nothing to forgive, Father!" Roger gasped, fighting to hold back his tears. "I'll get the wagon."

Roger flew to the stable. He hurriedly harnessed a donkey to a wagon and padded the wagon's bed with piles of fresh hay. By the time he returned, Brother Luke was kneeling beside Anthony. The friars were summoned and together they eased the dying priest onto the wagon. Roger jumped into the seat and took up the reins, urging the donkey into motion. Luke walked slowly beside the cart, holding Anthony's hand.

The road was full of stones and ruts. Roger tried his best to avoid them, but it was impossible. The wagon bumped and jerked at each turn of the wheels. The pitiless sun beat down on them. Not a breeze stirred the trees. Anthony's chest heaved painfully at every breath, but he was peaceful. "You know...Luke," he whispered, as the friar bent low to hear him, "I...was carried off...the Portuguese vessel...in Morocco...in something like this." Luke nodded. "When Philip...and I...landed in Sicily...I was brought...to the monastery...in a cart. And now...who knows?" Anthony smiled, "Maybe...the angels...will also...take me...to heaven...in a wagon!"

Luke forced himself to smile. "It's a thought, Father. It's a thought."

The tiny procession continued on in a silence broken only by Anthony's panting. They had gone about ten miles when Brother Roger saw a friar heading toward them. As he came closer, Roger recognized the color and form of his patched habit—he was a follower of Francis.

*"Maybe...the angels...will also...
take me...to heaven...in a wagon!"*

Roger pulled on the reins and halted the donkey. The friar ran up to the wagon. "Father Ignato!" Roger exclaimed.

"It's good to see you—" Ignato's voice broke off as he saw Anthony in the back of the wagon.

"We're on our way to Padua," Roger explained quietly. "He wants to die there."

Ignato came around the back of the wagon just as Brother Luke was gently tucking more straw under Anthony's head and shoulders. "This should help you to breathe easier, Father."

"Thank...you," Anthony struggled to say.

Ignato shut his eyes. It was too painful to see Anthony like this. *He'll never make it to Padua,* he thought. Ignato forced his eyes open and leaned over the wagon's side. "Anthony, it's Father Ignato."

Anthony lifted his hand. Ignato clasped it and pressed it to his chest. "Father, I have an idea. We're very close to the monastery of the Poor Ladies in Arcella. Let us take you there. You can rest for a while before continuing on to Padua."

Anthony weakly nodded and Ignato leapt into the seat beside Roger.

17

THE ARMS OF THE LORD

Within minutes the wagon pulled up beside the nuns' monastery. Ignato, Roger and Luke carried Anthony into the room reserved for the chaplain. They carefully laid him on a straw mattress.

Anthony's face and neck were beaded with perspiration. His body shook as he gasped desperately for air.

"Quick! Help me lift his head, Roger! He's choking!" Brother Luke shouted.

As the two struggled to raise Anthony's head, Father Ignato dragged a chair up to the bed. "We must get him to sit!" he yelled. "The water in his chest is rising!"

With one supporting his back and the other two taking him by the arms, the three friars pulled Anthony into a sitting position. Then they slid him into the chair.

By now the friars of Arcella had arrived. They knelt by the door in prayer. Soft voices echoed through the walls. The nuns were chanting the psalms for the dying.

Anthony's lips were moving, but no

words came out. Finally, he managed to whisper, "I'd like...to make...my confession."

Father Ignato drew closer and bent over the dying priest. After a few minutes, he straightened up and raised his hand in blessing "...and I absolve you of all your sins, in the name of the Father and of the Son and of the Holy Spirit."

"Amen," Anthony breathed fervently. He smiled as Father Ignato now brought him Jesus in Holy Communion. Anthony prayed silently for several long moments, then, to everyone's surprise, he began to softly sing a hymn to the Blessed Mother. The friars joined in. As the hymn ended, Anthony's eyes seemed fixed on a corner of the room. He continued to stare in amazement. His face was glowing with happiness. "What is it you see, Father?" Brother Roger whispered.

"Jesus...my...Savior!" Anthony gasped in wonder.

Father Ignato uncapped the container of holy oils he carried. Anthony held out his upturned palms. Ignato traced a cross on each of them as he began the Anointing of the Sick. Anthony murmured the prayers along with Ignato. The rest of the kneeling friars watched and prayed in silence.

As Ignato completed the anointing, the friars began to pray some of the psalms aloud. Anthony prayed with them. His voice was low, but clear. When the prayers ended, Anthony peacefully closed his eyes. His head relaxed back into Brother Roger's arms.

During the next half hour, his respiration worsened. The pauses between his deep breaths became longer and longer until his chest grew perfectly still. It was Ignato's deep voice that finally broke the silence. "Our Brother Anthony has passed into the loving arms of the Lord. Alleluia!"

"Alleluia!" the friars prayed.

18

ON THE LAMP STAND

The friars at Arcella knew how much the people of Padua loved Anthony. They also knew that many believed him to be a saint. The brothers realized that as soon as word of Anthony's death spread, the sisters' small monastery would be overrun. In the confusion of the moment, they decided to delay releasing the news.

But God had other plans. It is said that almost immediately after Anthony passed away, the children of Padua began running through the streets crying out, "Our Father Anthony is dead! Anthony, the saint, is dead!" The word spread like wildfire. Soon people from Padua and the neighboring towns were rushing toward Arcella.

When Roger heard a commotion outside, he pushed open the window shutter. A large crowd was already surrounding the monastery. Many were weeping. Others were begging to be allowed to pay their last respects to Anthony. "Brother Luke," he groaned, "it was Anthony's wish to be buried in Padua. How will we ever bring him there now?"

Luke ran his fingers through his hair. "I don't know. I just don't know."

"Brothers, quick! There's fighting outside!" a sister nervously called.

Luke rushed out to find two farmers grappling with each other. "Stop it! Please...I beg you to stop!" he cried. "What's wrong?"

The farmer from Arcella gave the man from Padua a rough shove. "The people of Padua would have us give them Anthony's body," he shouted, "but the saint died here and here he will stay!"

"Not so!" the second farmer yelled back. "Anthony always said he wanted to be buried in Padua and we've come to make sure that he is!"

Luke turned to face the crowd. "Good people!" he shouted, "You know that Father Anthony would never approve of this quarreling! The sisters and the people here would like Anthony to rest in Arcella. But his dying wish was to return to Padua. We'll bring the matter to the bishop and accept his decision. Whatever God wills will be done. But in the meantime," Luke's voice grew louder, "in the meantime, please show your love and respect for Father Anthony by returning peacefully to your homes. It's what he would want." A buzz ran through the crowd. Some of the people began to drift away. Others stubbornly refused to leave.

The next day, friars were sent from the Arcella monastery to the bishop. Upon hearing the news of Anthony's death and of the argument over where he should be buried, the bishop bowed his head in prayer. In a few moments he looked up. "To Padua, my Brothers, belongs the body of Father Anthony," he said slowly. "It was his desire to rest there and I feel certain God wishes us to honor that desire. I will come back with you myself. We will bring the body of Anthony from Arcella to Padua, walking in procession."

When the bishop arrived in Arcella on June 15, he announced the procession. Everyone who was able to was invited to join in the solemn event. The bishop's presence helped to calm some of the hurt and angry feelings that still remained.

Torches lit the gray morning and hymns filled the air as the procession escorting Anthony's body wound its way from Arcella to Padua. Small as it was, Saint Mary's Church in Padua extended its welcome to all the pilgrims. The bishop celebrated Mass there, after which Anthony was prayerfully laid to rest.

Soon after, the townspeople of Padua laid the foundation for a beautiful new church, to which they intended to move Anthony's body. People started praying to God through Anthony's intercession and miracles began to happen...cripples walked, the blind saw, the deaf heard and many returned to the practice of their faith.

"He was a saint!" people exclaimed. Day after day large crowds from nearby towns flocked to pray at Anthony's tomb. Before the year was up, the bishop and many of the priests and people had petitioned Pope Gregory IX to officially declare Anthony a saint.

Pope Gregory had known Anthony. He had witnessed the fire of God's love that burned in the young priest's heart. He knew that the miracles were proof of Anthony's holiness. Anthony's entire life had radiated goodness and love, bringing light to many people. The pope made up his mind. It was time to let the lamp of Anthony's life shine for people everywhere to see. It was time to place the lamp on a lamp stand.

On Pentecost Sunday, May 30, 1232, just short of the first anniversary of Anthony's death, Pope Gregory IX canonized him, establishing June 13 as Anthony's feast day. It was a special day of celebration for the whole Franciscan family. Francis of Assisi had been declared a saint only four years before. Now Anthony, who had loved and imitated Francis so closely, was also being greatly honored by the Church.

The canonization ceremony took place in the Italian town of Spoleto. Pope Gregory's voice rang out over the huge crowd of pilgrims packing the cathedral. "...Blessed Anthony, Light of Holy Church," the pope's voice grew stronger as he stretched out his arms toward heaven, "Lover of God's law, pray for us to Jesus!"

It was reported that on that day the bells in far-away Lisbon began ringing on their own, and the people of that city of Anthony's birth danced for joy. Their saint now belonged to the whole world.

Prayer

Saint Anthony, God was always first in your life. You loved him so much that you wanted all people everywhere to come to know, love and serve him too. You used your special talents for teaching and preaching to bring people closer to God, and to help those who were doubtful or confused.

There were many times in your life when things didn't work out as you had hoped for or expected, Saint Anthony. But you always trusted in God and in his love for you.

It's not always easy for me to put God first in my life. Would you please help me, Saint Anthony? Show me how I can use my gifts and talents to help the people around me. Help me to know and follow God's will and to trust that God never stops watching over and loving me.

I want to follow Jesus as you did. Pray for me, Saint Anthony.

Amen.

Glossary

1. Canonize—the act by which the Pope declares that a deceased person is a saint and may be honored by the whole Church. **Canonization** is the name given to the ceremony in which a person is declared a saint.

2. Cell—the small room of a friar, monk or nun.

3. Excommunicated—the word excommunicate means "to exclude from a community." When we say that a person is excommunicated, we mean that for some very, very serious reason he or she is not allowed to receive the sacraments, especially the Holy Eucharist.

4. Friar—a word meaning "brother." Friar is the name given to male members of certain religious Orders, such as the Franciscans and Dominicans. While a monk works and prays inside his monastery, a friar usually ministers to the People of God outside the monastery.

5. Fathers of the Church—holy men who lived during the early centuries of the Church. They preached and wrote to explain and sometimes also to defend the Christian Faith.

6. Hermit—a person who lives alone, devoting himself or herself to prayer.

7. Martyr—a person who allows himself or herself to be killed rather than to deny the Christian Faith.

8. Monastery—the place where friars, monks or nuns live as a community, dedicating themselves to a life of prayer.

9. Ordination—the ceremony in which a man receives the sacrament of Holy Orders. A man may be ordained a deacon, a priest or a bishop.

10. Poor Ladies—the name by which the Poor Clare nuns were originally called. This order of nuns was founded by Saint Clare, under the direction of Saint Francis of Assisi.

11. Superior—the name given to the person who governs a religious community. Among the Franciscan friars, superiors are also called guardians. A provincial superior is responsible for a group of several religious communities which make up a division of the religious Order. This group of communities is called a **province.**

BOOKS & MEDIA

The Daughters of St. Paul operate book and media centers at the following addresses. Visit, call or write the one nearest you today, or find us on the World Wide Web, www.pauline.org

CALIFORNIA

3908 Sepulveda Blvd, Culver City, CA 90230	310-397-8676
5945 Balboa Avenue, San Diego, CA 92111	858-565-9181
46 Geary Street, San Francisco, CA 94108	415-781-5180

FLORIDA

145 S.W. 107th Avenue, Miami, FL 33174	305-559-6715

HAWAII

1143 Bishop Street, Honolulu, HI 96813	808-521-2731
Neighbor Islands call:	800-259-8463

ILLINOIS

172 North Michigan Avenue, Chicago, IL 60601	312-346-4228

LOUISIANA

4403 Veterans Memorial Blvd, Metairie, LA 70006	504-887-7631

MASSACHUSETTS

885 Providence Hwy, Dedham, MA 02026	781-326-5385

MISSOURI

9804 Watson Road, St. Louis, MO 63126	314-965-3512

NEW JERSEY

561 U.S. Route 1, Wick Plaza, Edison, NJ 08817	732-572-1200

NEW YORK

150 East 52nd Street, New York, NY 10022	212-754-1110

PENNSYLVANIA

9171-A Roosevelt Blvd, Philadelphia, PA 19114	215-676-9494

SOUTH CAROLINA

243 King Street, Charleston, SC 29401	843-577-0175

TENNESSEE

4811 Poplar Avenue, Memphis, TN 38117	901-761-2987

TEXAS

114 Main Plaza, San Antonio, TX 78205	210-224-8101

VIRGINIA

1025 King Street, Alexandria, VA 22314	703-549-3806

CANADA

3022 Dufferin Street, Toronto, ON M6B 3T5	416-781-9131

¡También somos su fuente para libros, videos y música en español!